science fair winners

CRIME SCENE SCIENCE

20 projects and experiments about
clues, crimes, criminals, and other
mysterious things

by Karen Romano Young

Illustrations by David Goldin

NATIONAL GEOGRAPHIC

WASHINGTON, D.C.

credits

All illustration by David Goldin

PUBLISHED BY THE NATIONAL GEOGRAPHIC SOCIETY

John M. Fahey, Jr., *President and Chief Executive Officer*
Gilbert M. Grosvenor, *Chairman of the Board*
Tim T. Kelly, President, *Global Media Group*
John Q. Griffin, *Executive Vice President; President, Publishing*
Nina D. Hoffman, *Executive Vice President; President, Book Publishing Group*
Melina Gerosa Bellows, *Executive Vice President, Children's Publishing*

PREPARED BY THE BOOK DIVISION

Nancy Laties Feresten, *Vice President, Editor in Chief, Children's Books*
Jonathan Halling, *Design Director, Children's Publishing*
Jennifer Emmett, *Executive Editor, Children's Books*
Carl Mehler, *Director of Maps*
R. Gary Colbert, *Production Director*
Jennifer A. Thornton, *Managing Editor*

STAFF FOR THIS BOOK

Amy Shields, Priyanka Lamichhane, *Project Editors*
Bea Jackson, Director of Design and Illustration
James Hiscott, Jr., *Art Director / Designer*
Grace Hill, *Associate Managing Editor*
Lewis R. Bassford, *Production Manager*
Susan Borke, *Legal and Business Affairs*

MANUFACTURING AND QUALITY MANAGEMENT

Christopher A. Liedel, *Chief Financial Officer*
Phillip L. Schlosser, *Vice President*
Chris Brown, *Technical Director*
Nicole Elliott, *Manager*
Rachel Faulise, *Manager*

Many of the projects in this book involve human or animal subjects. The International Science and Engineering Fair (ISEF) rules include specific requirements for these types of projects. Students should familiarize themselves generally with the ISEF rules as well as the rules specific to animal and human subjects. Students also need to complete all necessary documents to ensure their project complies with the ISEF requirements. Students who have questions should seek clarification from their teachers.

You can find additional information on the ISEF website:
www.societyforscience.org/isef/about/index.asp
www.societyforscience.org/isef/rules/rules7.pdf
www.societyforscience.org/isef/rules/rules10.pdf

For more information, please call 1-800-NGS LINE (647-5463) or write to the following address:
National Geographic Society
1145 17th Street N.W.
Washington, D.C. 20036-4688 U.S.A.

Visit us online at www.nationalgeographic.com/books

For librarians and teachers: www.ngchildrensbooks.org

More for kids from National Geographic:
kids.nationalgeographic.com

For information about special discounts for bulk purchases, please contact National Geographic Books Special Sales: ngspecsales@ngs.org

For rights or permissions inquiries, please contact National Geographic Books Subsidiary Rights: ngbookrights@ngs.org

Library of Congress Cataloging-in-Publication Data
Young, Karen Romano.
  Science fair winners : crime scene science : 20 projects and experiments about clues, crimes, criminals, and other mysterious things / by Karen Romano Young ; illustrations by David Goldin.
    p. cm.
  Includes bibliographical references and index.
  ISBN 978-1-4263-0521-4 (pbk : alk. paper) -- ISBN 978-1-4263-0522-1 (library binding : alk. paper)
 1. Criminal investigation--Juvenile literature. 2. Crime scenes--Juvenile literature. 3. Forensic sciences--Juvenile literature. 4. Science projects--Juvenile literature. I. Title.
  HV8073.Y68 2009
  363.325--dc22
                    2009020387
Printed in U.S.A.
09/WOR/1

THE WORKSHOPS

WELCOME TO CRIME SCENE SCIENCE

the introduction

Crime Scene Science is dedicated to helping you design a science project that will make your teachers and judges love you—and that grows out of your own interests, passions, and goals.

Here you'll be able to get inside the head—and toolbox—of modern-day experts as they detect, collect, inspect, and connect without being detected, expected, dissected, or rejected.

One of the first things the police do when they race to the scene of a crime is to hang yellow crime scene tape around the area where the action happened. Why do they do this? For one reason: to protect the clues. Fingerprints, footprints, DNA samples, blood, wreckage, debris, and other evidence could lead detectives to the criminal. The data they get from studying this stuff helps detectives and forensic scientists understand what happened, when it happened, how it happened, and even why it happened.

The point of this book is to put you inside that yellow tape so you can figure out what evidence needs to be collected and inspected to get the maximum information out of a crime scene, suspect, or artifact. The workshops give you scientific tools for examining data so that you can take a simple question—What happened here?—and study it through observation, comparison, and conclusion (the building blocks of the scientific method). You'll also find tips on doing your own research, finding a mentor, and learning about the field of science that is connected with your project.

And we'll introduce you to people at work in the fields of forensic science (biology, archaeology, entomology, and the rest), psychology, law, technology, and even theater arts so that you get the broadest understanding of what a 21st-century detective needs to know. But we won't leave it there. We'll show you how to present your project—in the classroom, at a science fair, on the Web, and in writing, art, and performance.

You'll love the response you get to your *Crime Scene Science* project. And don't be surprised if you find yourself seeing the true stories behind everyday objects and innocent faces—and figuring out some new plots yourself.

about science

Here's what a scientist needs:
- the ability to notice things

What kinds of things? In these workshops, it's physical evidence. Visible things, of course, but also invisible things, from microscopic objects to memories.

- the ability to answer questions

What kinds of questions? Questions that lead to actions, such as:

What if...?

I wonder...?

How can I find out...?

These three question starters are the start of all science. They lead to observing, experimenting, reaching a conclusion, and finding another question, which leads you to more science and more watching, testing, and understanding, which leads to another question. Well, you get the idea.

which workshop?

Some of them are experiments. This is great because lots of science fairs require you to do an experiment. Some of them aren't experiments. This is because real scientists don't just do experiments (and some science fairs don't require them). Sure, experiments are important. But much of real science falls into two categories: observation and surveying.

You make observations when you find a footprint, check the weather, or try to figure out how long ago a footprint was made.

You survey when you look to see what other footprints there are, count the different feet they represent, and figure out the pattern of foot traffic through an area. In other words, you repeat your observation to see if it reveals a trend.

You experiment when you change something in a situation and observe and survey the outcome. For example, you might change the placement of lights in a store's parking lot and watch how this changes the pattern of car and foot traffic

ogy (what's going on in someone's head), sociology (how a group and members of a group behave), anthropology (the study of human culture), and economics (the science of money and business).

Some of the workshops seem hard, and others seem easy. This might depend on what you find easy to do and what makes you nervous. It's all good science, based on real studies and experiments. If you're not sure whether a workshop will satisfy your teacher's requirements, ask him or her before getting started.

what is forensics?

It's proof. Forensic scientists make observations and gather data for the purpose of finding a criminal and providing the evidence needed to convince a jury or judge of the culprit's guilt or innocence. But the work of a forensic scientist doesn't always involve a crime. It involves finding and using clues to get to the bottom of any situation—whether it's the diet of an ancient Egyptian and his cat, the path a runaway dog took through a city, or the identity of someone crossing an international border.

Forensics is the science of finding clues—a spy's or detective's job—and of understanding what information those clues can give. Today's forensic

into the store.

Scientists often make discoveries by studying their data. Imagine that you have a list of global positions and headings for a car. You note that the positions and headings of the car repeat as you go down the list. You realize that the car was traveling in circles. This leads you to ask a new question: What was the driver looking for or waiting for?

Some of the workshops seem really science-y. Some of them don't. This might be because you define science in terms of biology (the study of life), chemistry (the elements), or physics (time, space, and motion). But this book includes workshops that look at clues through the eyes of social scientists, too. Social science includes psychol-

scientists analyze clues and work to find new clues or new ways to use clues we already know about.

what is detective work?

In the United States and many other countries, a crime suspect is considered innocent until he or she is proven guilty. So gathering proof—evidence that adds up to support convicting a suspect of having committed a crime—is the job of the detective at a crime scene. A detective is a puzzle solver who puts together the pieces—tiny clues, events, or other pieces of information—to make a story about what happened. Detectives have learned not only to rely on the clues they can observe at a crime scene, but also to gather materials that can be analyzed by forensic scientists, people who specialize in "making

evidence talk"—linking information to suspects.

But detectives studying crimes need to be students of human nature, as well, so that they can read a criminal's actions in clues while connecting motivations, methods, and means (the three M's that make someone a crime suspect). They also use this information to draw confessions out of guilty parties.

Often, the outcome is surprising. Detectives say that it is important to be open to all that you can take in through all your senses—including a sixth sense some law enforcers have that leads them to feel that something's just not right.

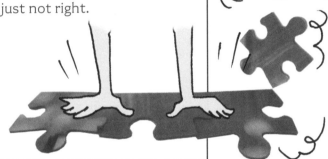

If you want to become a forensic scientist, don't just watch the TV shows... forensic scientists don't really make a million dollars a year.

—Dr. Henry Lee, *forensic scientist*

CASE OF MISTAKEN IDENTITY

(Examine fingerprints)

TIME NEEDED >
three days

SCIENCE >
anatomy and physiology,
genetics, biometrics

SCIENCE CONCEPT >
patterns

ADULT INVOLVEMENT >
use of ink, paint,
powders, or other
substances to transfer
fingerprints

the basics

UNLIKE OTHER PARTS of the skin, the fingertips have friction ridges, which let us grip. Even between identical twins, fingerprints (impressions made by those ridges) are never exactly alike, so your fingerprint is one way to differentiate you from the rest of humankind. The practice of using fingerprints for identification is called *dactyloscopy*.

the buzz

Disney World began using biometrics to check the identity of ticket holders in 1996, and their technology has improved as scientists have learned more. They used to need two fingerprints; now they just need one.

the lingo

biometrics—technology that allows people to be identified based on physical features

you'll need

black pencil
charcoal—artist charcoal or from the fireplace
printer paper
clear tape—either scotch tape or packing tape
kids from your classroom
ink pad and roller (optional)

A FEW METHODS OF FINGERPRINTING:

A. Use a soft, dark pencil or piece of charcoal to draw a dark, shiny spot about the size of a quarter on piece of printer paper. Rub your fingertip on the shape until it is covered with carbon. Have a helper stick a piece of tape directly on your finger, being careful not to touch the sticky part of the tape

the QUESTION >> How can fingerprints be used to identify people and learn more about them—and to solve crimes?

the PLAN >> Gather and study fingerprints and design your own system for analyzing them.

or your finger, and being careful not to smudge your fingertip with the tape. Have the helper lift the tape carefully and stick it onto a fresh sheet of printer paper. Label the paper with your name and the finger you used.

B. Take a piece of charcoal and crumble it finely or grate it over a clean cookie sheet, shaking the sheet to spread the charcoal around. Press your fingertips onto the cookie sheet at different points in the charcoal. Then use wide, clear tape (such as packing tape) to lift the fingerprints off the cookie sheet. Carefully place the tape on printer paper to preserve the charcoal-outlined fingerprints. **NOTE:** *You may get a better print by placing a small amount of hand lotion or olive oil on your hands before pressing your fingertips onto the cookie sheet.*

C. Use an ink pad. Roll your fingertip around on it and then press your finger onto paper. Experiment with the pressure and amount of ink.

what to do

1 **IMAGINE** that you are the first person ever to discover the characteristics of fingerprints. It will be your job to explain this phenomenon to others. Begin by taking fingerprints from an assortment of people—your class is a great place to start—and then analyzing them. Come up with names for the similar features, patterns, and textures you discover.

2 **COUNT** how many people in your study share each feature.

3 **CREATE** several enlarged fingerprints in order to display the features you have discovered and named. You might do this by taking a digital photograph of a print and then using your computer to enlarge it. You can also take the print to a copy store to enlarge it.

4 **LINK PEOPLE'S NAMES** to their fingerprints in order to understand the groups that share features. Do they have other characteristics in common besides the shared features of their fingerprints? Come up with a questionnaire that will provide you with the data you want in order to group people. Consider factors such as age, gender, race, origin, and family.

5 **COMPARE THE DATA** you have gathered. Do people who share fingerprint features share other features as well?

WORKSHOP RESOURCE >>
Come On In, Ed German's website about fingerprints and other biometrics: www.onin.com

CONSIDER THIS! PRESENT THIS!

What group of people would you guess had shared fingerprint features, based on your classroom study of kids who are not related to each other but are close to the same age? Who else's fingerprints would you like to look at in order to answer the question?

In your science fair display, include a diagram showing different fingerprint characteristics, along with a graph showing other factors shared by people who have this characteristic. Set up a station where you can take additional fingerprints to add to your study. You might consider including a magnifying lens so people can compare their fingerprint features with those in your data set.

GO THE EXTRA MILE! Experiment with using a computer scanner to photograph people's fingertips. Would this work as a less messy method for collecting information for identification?

FIRST IMPRESSIONS

(Make castings or prints at a crime scene)

TIME NEEDED >
one day

SCIENCE >
physics, geology,
mathematics

SCIENCE CONCEPTS >
physics of density and
displacement, materials,
patterns and attributes

ADULT INVOLVEMENT >
You may need an adult
to help you walk over
sand, clay, dirt, or other
surfaces.

the basics

FROM STUDYING SOMEONE'S SHOE PRINT, detectives can infer speed of movement (at what angle was the print pressed into the ground?), economic level (how old is the suspect's shoe?), activities (was it a workboot or a ballet shoe?), gender, age, and much more.

negative print—a shoe print left in a substance such as dust, mud, or snow

positive print—a dirty shoeprint left on a surface such as linoleum or tile

you'll need

camera

casting material—plaster of paris or dental stone, 1 pound per casting

sealed container—marked in five-ml measures, filled with water

shoes—three different pairs for the adult subject to wear

one-gallon freezer storage bags

sturdy cardboard box

tweezers

hair spray or spray fixative—from an art supply store

optional:

vaseline

paint powder—from an art supply or craft store

vinyl or latex gloves

flexible cardboard

potassium sulfate—can be ordered online with parent's permission

QUESTION >>

What can the shape, pattern, and texture of a shoe tell you about the perpetrator of a crime?

PLAN >>

Make an impression of a shoe and attempt to find its match by examining tread, wear, size, and any other identifying features.

the buzz

In February 2007, British investigators announced a new service: Footwear Intelligence Technology, a database containing the images of the soles of thousands of shoes. It was created to give forensic scientists a leg up in finding criminals who left their footprints behind, then hoofed it out of there.

what to do

1 **ASK AN ADULT TO CREATE** a mystery impression. He or she should walk through an area where the ground (dirt or sand) is somewhat soft. You should NOT be there when this happens. The purpose is for the adult to provide you with mystery prints, wearing shoes you don't see.

2 MAKE A CAST OR PHOTO-GRAPH OF EACH PRINT.

Photograph any print less than 1/4-inch deep. See *Picture This*, p. 73, for instructions. Cast prints more than 1/4-inch deep. This is because the imprints are too deep for photographs to capture their details clearly.

A. Freezer storage bags with one-gallon capacity can hold enough dry casting material for a tire imprint or footprint. Measure ahead, and determine how much water you'll need to add to the pre-measured plaster. On site, you can pour the water straight into the bag, mix by kneading the sealed bag, and check that the consistency of the casting compound stays as liquid and mushy as cake batter.

B. Check the condition of your impression for crumbling sand, leaves, bugs, etc. Remove small items with tweezers. Spray a light shot of hair spray or spray fixative into the impression. This will hold it in place while you make your cast.

C. Pour the casting material into the impression from the side, so that it slides gently into the imprint from the force of gravity. Pouring casting material directly onto a detail such as writing, logos, or other fine patterning can destroy its clarity and make it impossible for you to identify the item.

D. Let the cast set for 20 minutes or more. The colder it is, the longer you should let the cast set.

E. Remove the cast by digging the entire impression out gently with your fingers. Place it in the cardboard box.

F. Let the cast dry overnight so that it is completely firm inside and out.

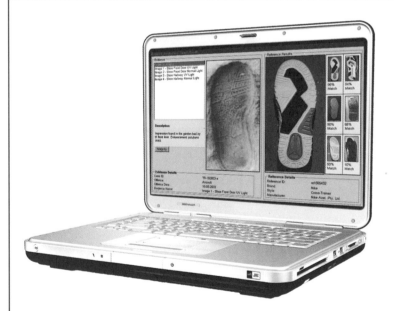

Does it match? Students at La Trobe University, in Australia, created a database of shoes that were uniquely Australian as an aid for forensic scientists.

> ""
> **(When I was a kid) I had a tracking box in my bedroom. That's a box of sand that I walked in, pretending I was an animal. The sand determined how my tracks would look if I turned or walked backward.**
> ""

—TV archaeologist Josh Bernstein
as told to Stacey Stowe of the New York Times

CONSIDER THIS! PRESENT THIS!

> How could you use footprints and castings to learn more about animals?

> Include your analysis of the prints or casts and the criteria you used to identify a shoe. What measurements and comparisons did you make? What conclusions did you arrive at?

Optional: If you use dental stone to make your cast, it may be brushed gently with a solution of potassium sulfate mixed with water to clean it.

How to make a positive print:

A. Place a latex glove on your hand and spread vaseline thinly and evenly onto the sole of the shoe. If you are allergic to latex, use a vinyl glove.

B. Walk the shoe gently and firmly across the cardboard, rolling from heel to toe, as if the shoe were on a walking person.

C. Sprinkle paint powder onto the vaseline to make the print visible.

Another option is to ink the shoe tread with black printing ink, using a printing roller. (Both these items are available at art supply stores.)

3 **ATTEMPT TO MATCH** your cast with a photograph or print of the sole of the shoe. Your adult helper may photograph a variety of similar shoes to test your observing skills.

WORKSHOP RESOURCE >>
Footwear: The Missed Evidence 2d ed. by Dwane S. Hilderbrand. Staggs Publishing, 2007.

THE SOLES ARE THE WINDOW TO THE BODY

(Predict a suspect's height)

the basics

FROM FOOTPRINTS, detectives and professional trackers can infer height, weight, gender, direction, speed, and gait (a person's rhythm and pattern of walking).

TIME NEEDED >
two or three days

SCIENCE >
anatomy and physiology, math

SCIENCE CONCEPTS >
proportions, scale, scientific method

ADULT INVOLVEMENT >
none

the buzz

Ray Wallace created a large set of footprints in 1958 in the hope of scaring off criminals. Before he knew it, news went out that the Bigfoot of Native American legend was still around. People's assumption was that big footprints meant a big critter. After Wallace's death in 2002, his family revealed that the footprints were a hoax. But many people still go on hunts for Bigfoot, or Sasquatch, as he is called by some.

the QUESTION >>

Can you use a person's footprint to predict height as a way of gathering information about the identification of a crime suspect?

the PLAN >>

Measure people's feet and compare their foot's length with their height, working to see if you can look at somebody's footprint and figure out how tall he or she is.

the lingo

ratio—the relationship between two or more numbers as expressed as the quotient of one divided by the other. For example, the ratio of height and arm span is usually 1:1 because the measurements are usually the same. A ratio in which one number was twice the other would be written as 2:1.

you'll need

people's feet
metric metal measuring tape—you can use a cloth measuring tape or ruler if you have to
chalk
calculator

NOTE: *Begin with 20 people. Later, you may determine that you need more data—and more feet. Try to choose adults of the same gender in order to control your data. Later, you can experiment with different genders and ages to figure out whether there are different ratios for them.*

what to do

1 **MEASURE** 20 subjects' foot length and height. Use metric numbers; you're a scientist!

2 **FIND THE RATIO.** For each set of measurements, divide the height by the foot measurement to get a decimal number that represents the ratio of height to foot length.

3 **COMPARE THE OUTCOMES.**
How close is the ratio of one person's measurements to that of another? What is the margin of error? Find the average of all of your ratios. **NOTE**: *It might help to plot the ratios on a graph. You'll see the curve—in which the average of the ratios is the highest point—and outliers, or unusual results, fall in lower numbers to the right or left of the curve depending on whether they're higher or lower than the average.*

4 **CREATE A FORMULA** based on the average ratio you found. For example, say your average ratio is 6:1, meaning that a person's height is six times his foot length. If you know that, then you can figure out the person's height even if you only have his foot length.

5 **GATHER** only foot measurements from another group of people.

6 **USE YOUR FORMULA** to predict the height of each person.

7 **MEASURE** the height of the people in the group. Do their heights fall inside your margin of error? How can you adjust your formula to be more exact?

Compare the information you gathered in this study with what you could learn from Workshop 2. If you had the bare footprint of a suspect, would it help you find him or her? How do the lengths of shoe prints vary from bare footprints? Do the ratio and formula change when you have shoe prints instead of bare footprints?

CONSIDER THIS! PRESENT THIS!

A spreadsheet program can make a clear presentation of your measurement data.

GO THE EXTRA MILE! Try using your ratios with subjects of different ages and genders. Or see if you can come up with a ratio for a different animal species.

WORKSHOP RESOURCE >>

For help with ratios, visit Math Forum:
www.mathforum.org

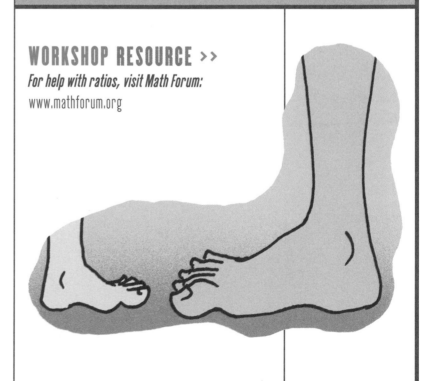

MAPPING THE SCENE

(Connect the dots of crime scenes)

TIME NEEDED >
one week to ten days

SCIENCE >
geography, sociology

SCIENCE CONCEPTS >
geographic information systems (GIS), current events, cause and effect, analysis of patterns, profiling

ADULT INVOLVEMENT >
You'll need an adult to accompany and/or drive you to the areas you study.

the basics

GEOGRAPHIC INFORMATION SYSTEMS (GIS),** in which statistics can be plotted on a map, have transformed how scientists, economists, retailers, traffic analysts, law enforcement officials, detectives, and others analyze the way people live and why events occur when and where they do.

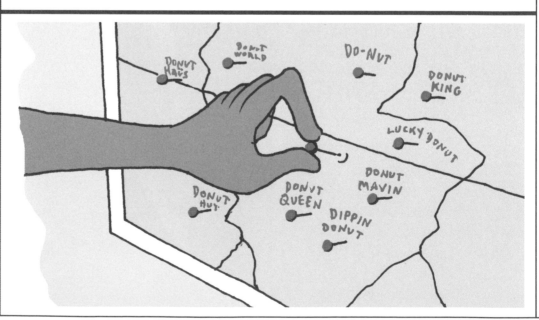

the buzz

Maps of crime scenes have led to changes in traffic patterns, police patrols, store operation hours, and even the lights used outside businesses. COMPSTAT (short for Computer Statistics) began in New York City in 1994. It collects and delivers information about the crime in an area for police officers. COMPSTAT has led to less crime in many areas.

the lingo

profiling—analyzing a crime according to people, places, and things in order to try to understand the circumstances or conditions that may contribute to it

you'll need

news source—daily newspaper, police blotter, or other news source that gives local crime data
map of your town or neighborhood
marker or colored pencils

what to do

1 **FOLLOW NEWS REPORTS OF CRIMES.** Keep track of the types of crimes (break-ins, personal robberies or muggings, vandalism, etc.), the time of day each occurred, the places, and information about the victims and suspects, if any.

2 **CREATE A CODING SYSTEM** using colors or icons (symbols) to show different types of crimes.

3 **PLACE A COLOR DOT** or icon on the map at the scene of each crime and note the time of the crime.

the QUESTION >> How does a map change the way you see crime data?

the PLAN >> Use newspapers or other local news sources to create a list of the times, scenes, and types of crimes committed in a town or neighborhood for a week or longer. Then transfer these data to a map and interpret the patterns you observe.

4 **LOOK FOR PATTERNS.** When you have mapped all the crimes for a period of time (days or weeks), study the map. Use these questions to guide you as well as others that come to your mind:
- Do certain kinds of crimes occur more or less often than others?
- What can you observe about the times when crimes occur?

> How could you get more information about the area? For example, can you interview local law enforcement officers? Have other GIS studies been done in the area over a longer period of time? If so, could you compare them with your own work?

CONSIDER THIS! PRESENT THIS!

> Make a website that includes your map and other information about the area you studied, including safety tips and recommendations.

> **GO THE EXTRA MILE!** Use ArcGIS Explorer or another digital GIS program that allows you to input data into a map. See Resources, this page. Check with the math, science, and geography teachers at your school to see who might be able to help with GIS.

• What pattern do you see in the places where crimes occur?

What can you conclude based on the patterns you observed?

5 **INVESTIGATE.** With an adult, visit the areas you mapped that interest you most. What information can you add to your understanding of the pattern you observed? What do you notice about the outdoor lighting? About the businesses and buildings? About natural factors such as trees?

6 **RESULTS.** Can you recommend changes that might improve the safety of the area you studied?

WORKSHOP RESOURCES >>

Download ArcGIS Explorer: www.esri.com

Watch the demos to see how to use ArcGIS to add local data to existing maps: http://www.esri.com/software/arcgis/explorer/demos.html

Crime Maps and COMPSTAT, the Los Angeles Police Department crime mapping system: http://www.lapdonline.org/crime_maps_and_compstat

To see crimes reported in your area and to compare your area to others: www.CrimeReports.com

HIDE ME!

(Experiment with the principles of the cloak of invisibility)

the basics

LIGHT REACHES YOUR EYE through photons, little bits of energy that combine into waves. Not all light is visible; just a small range of waves appears as colors that the eye can perceive. Invisible light includes microwaves and radar waves, as well as infrared and ultraviolet light.

TIME NEEDED >
one day

SCIENCE >
physics

SCIENCE CONCEPTS >
electromagnetic spectrum, properties of light

ADULT INVOLVEMENT >
none

the buzz

David R. Smith and David Schurig of Duke University in North Carolina are working on creating a system of using microwaves to coat metal and keep it from being detected by radar. Preliminary work successfully hid a flat piece of metal, making it "the first functional invisibility cloak," reported *Science News* in late 2006. Now Smith and Schurig are experimenting with making the "cloak" work on a three-dimensional object. Their method relies on bending light waves, more like the way Marvel Comics' Invisible Woman is able to turn light waves away from her body than the way Harry Potter uses his cloak of invisibility in the famous J. K. Rowling books.

NOTE: *What's stealth? The idea is not to be detected by radar. There are two ways to do this: 1) You can make an object absorb radio waves rather than reflect them back to the radar detector; 2) You can make an object reflect radio waves not to the radar station, but to other places. This is like positioning a mirror so it doesn't show you your own image, but shows you the ceiling or floor instead.*

> **"**
> *Unlike traditional stealth, an invisibility cloak reduced both reflection and shadow. Thus both these ways of detecting an object... are weakened.*
> **"**
>
> —David Schurig
> *address at Virginia Tech, March 2007*

the lingo

reflection—the action of light waves that return from a surface at the same angle at which they entered

refraction—the action of light waves that bend as they travel through something

you'll need

a container—fish tank (20 gallons or larger)

water resistant objects—different shapes and sizes

laser pointer

the QUESTION >>
Can light be refracted to change the way things look?

the PLAN >>
Simple light experiments let you see the properties of light waves being used by scientists to make a cloak of invisibility.

mirror
spoon
pencil
**fabrics, wraps, screening, film
screen** (optional)

what to do

The start of any invention is using what you know as a jumping-off point to the unknown. In this workshop you'll begin with a set of observations and experiments that show how light can change the way an image reaches your eye. You can jump off this set into a demonstration of how light travels, or you can make conceptual drawings of cloaks of invisibility using the principles you've discovered. You can stop there, or you can choose one cloak concept and plan its development.

1 CHANGING LIGHT. This set of observations and experiments shows how light can change the way the image of an object reaches the eye.

A. Fill the fish tank with water. Drop in a few objects of different shapes and sizes. Looking only from the side, reach into the top and try to grab each object. Can you do it on the first try?

B. Dip the pencil into the water halfway. Look at the pencil from different angles: from above, from the side, and up through the water from the bottom. What happens to the image of the straight pencil when seen through water?

C. Hang a piece of paper on the wall so you can see it through the fish tank. Shine the laser pointer through the water and mark the spot on the wall where the light falls. Experiment with mirrors and spoons to reflect the light beam and change the angle at which it passes through the water.

D. Now add a few drops of milk to the water. Aim the laser pointer through the water. Does the laser point on the wall change? What if you add even more milk to the water?

E. Experiment with shining light on and through different materials besides water: film screens, foil, wraps, and fabrics. What happens to the light?

2 ADD MATERIALS AND SITUATIONS YOU THINK OF YOURSELF.
Use your knowledge of how light,

materials, and images work to create concepts for a cloak of invisibility.

For example, say you designed a cloak of fabric that could receive images the way a computer screen does. What kinds of images would the cloak have to receive in order to make the person wearing it seem invisible? What effect would a cloak that used water, screening, foils, wraps, fabrics, or other materials have? The key to coming up with a concept is to design it without knowing exactly how it works, basing your design on your observation of scientific or technical phenomena.

3 **PICK THE CONCEPT** that you think is the strongest or most interesting, and draw the cloak of invisibility. Label your design with descriptions of the features and workings of the cloak. This will raise plenty of questions.

4 **RESEARCH** ways in which the questions might be answered in terms of invention, further research, or consultation with experts. For example, if you are worried that the person wearing the cloak of invisibility will cast a shadow even though he can't be seen, consider how that shadow might be eliminated.

WORKSHOP RESOURCE >>
"The Science Fact and Fiction of Invisibility"
by David R. Smith, Duke University:
http://people.ee.duke.edu/~drsmith/cloaking.html

> What would you use a cloak of invisibility for? Could the police use one?

CONSIDER THIS! PRESENT THIS!

> Create a demonstration of your materials and the way they interact with light and images. One way to do this is to use flat or curved mirrors to send one laser light through a series of materials until it hits a bull's-eye on your demonstration table or a nearby wall.

> **GO THE EXTRA MILE!** Create a development plan for building and testing a prototype cloak of invisibility. What materials would you need? What facilities? What advice? What money?

DUDE, WHERE'S MY DOG?

(Teach bloodhound techniques to your dog)

the basics

DOGS HAVE THE ABILITY to learn how to play games and understand language. They have a hearing range much greater than that of humans and a terrific sense of smell. All of these characteristics make dogs the perfect pet detectives.

TIME NEEDED >
two or three weeks

SCIENCE >
animal physiology and behavior

SCIENCE CONCEPTS >
behavior modification, law enforcement and detective techniques, forming hypotheses

ADULT INVOLVEMENT >
You'll need adult permission—and possibly a helper—as you train your dog.

the buzz

Kat Albrecht used to be a police detective who worked at finding missing persons. She was in charge of training dogs to find people, but she grew frustrated over how little she and her dogs were called on to work. So she began teaching her own dog, Rachel, to look for lost pets. Now she has become the first licensed pet detective. She founded Pet Hunters International (PHI), an academy that teaches people—and dogs!—to find lost pets. Here are some of PHI's methods for finding lost pets:

- using amplified listening devices, night vision binoculars, baby monitors, the bionic ear, and other devices that let detectives see and hear what's happening at remote sites—especially places where lost pets would hide
- predicting distances an animal might travel
- search probability theory (identifying places an animal is most likely to go)
- tracking (following footprints)
- lost pet forensics: collection and analysis of physical evidence (hair, feces, bones, whiskers, etc.)

the lingo

behavior modification—a technique that uses rewards and punishments to change the way a person or animal acts

insider info

HomeAgain Pet Recovery Service reports that only 16 percent of dogs and 2 percent of cats find their way home again once they are lost.

you'll need

a dog
a collar
hot dogs
garlic powder and cheddar cheese
sterile gauze pads
a clicker—a training tool available at pet stores
a helper
a photographer or videographer—to record your activities
a journal

---

the QUESTION >> Can you teach your dog to find and track a scent?

the PLAN >> This workshop is the beginning of PHI's scent training, during which dogs learn to search out lost people and pets. It uses positive reinforcement, a behavior modification method in which a person or pet is taught to do what you want through rewards for good behavior.

what to do

As you do this workshop, have someone photograph or video what you do. In your journal, make notes about the time of each training session, what you do, and the results.

1 **TEACH YOUR DOG THAT THE CLICK MEANS A TREAT.** He'll learn that the click is praise.
- Cut hot dog circles (HDC) by slicing the hot dog crosswise.
- Give your dog a HDC at the exact moment you click the clicker.
- Do this in five-minute sessions for two or three days until he gets that a click means "good dog!"

2 **TEACH THE DOG TO SEARCH VISUALLY FOR THE HDC.** He'll learn that "SEARCH" means he's going to get a treat. In this step, he's just seeing the object he's searching for.
- Hold the HDC in your throwing hand.
- Hold the dog by the collar with the other hand. You might also have a friend or an adult hold the dog by the collar.
- Throw the HDC where the dog can still see it.
- At the precise moment you let go of the collar, say, "SEARCH!"
- When he gets to the HDC, praise him and click the clicker.

- Do this for two 5-minute sessions a day until he gets it.

3 **TEACH THE DOG TO FIND THE HDC.** He'll learn that "SEARCH" means he's going to find something and get a treat. In this step, he can't see the object he's searching for.
- Hold the HDC in your throwing hand.
- Hold the dog by the collar with the other hand, or have someone else hold him.
- Get him excited by saying, "READY? READY?"
- Throw the HDC behind the couch or into some tall weeds.
- At the precise moment you let go

of the collar, say, "SEARCH!"
- As he finds the HDC, praise him and click.

4 **TEACH THE DOG TO FIND AN HDC BY SCENT.** From this step on, you need a helper.
- Have your helper hold the dog by his collar.
- Rub the HDC onto a sterile gauze pad.
- Throw the HDC into a hidden spot.
- Hold the gauze pad under his nose. As he sniffs it, say, "SNIFF!"

- Say, "READY? READY?"
- At the precise moment the helper lets go of the collar, say, "SEARCH!"
- As he finds the HDC, praise him and click.

5 **TEACH THE DOG TO FIND A HDC WITHOUT SEEING YOU THROW IT.** Covering his eyes helps him transition to looking for something he hasn't watched you hide.
- Rub the HDC on a sterile gauze pad.
- Have your helper hold the dog by the collar and cover the dog's eyes with his or her hand.
- Throw the HDC into a hidden spot.
- Repeat the last 4 steps from experiment 4 above

WORKSHOP RESOURCES >>

How to Train Your Dog to Locate Lost Pets
by Kat Albrecht (Dogwise, 2007)

The Lost Pet Chronicles: Adventures of a K-9 Cop Turned Pet Dectective
by Kat Albrecht (Bloomsbury, 2004)

Missing Pet Partnership:
www.lostapet.org

Kat Albrecht's Website:
www.katalbrecht.com

How would you train your dog to find your brother or sister?

This workshop is the perfect subject for a video. Speed it up to take less presentation time, and add to the fun.

GO THE EXTRA MILE! You can teach your dog to track your cat by its scent. (Use your own cat. Don't teach your dog to find it if the two pets don't already have a good relationship!) Rub a sterile gauze pad over your cat. Then hide the cat in its carrier, and follow step 5 with the cat-scented pad. But how will you keep the cat quiet? Read on.

Get the cat's carrier and place it outside, without the cat in it. Throw birdseed and bread crumbs around the empty carrier to attract birds. After the birds are used to coming for food all around the cat carrier, place the cat in the carrier. A cat's instinctive response to being in the middle of all these birds is to be quiet.

YO! WHODUNNIT?

(Test observational memories)

the basics

SEARCH AND RESCUE TEAMS are usually led by police departments or park services. Search teams rely on witnesses' observations to send them in the right direction. Who saw the person last? What was the person wearing? Were there other people in the area? What was the weather like? What time of day was it? Specific observations lead to a better search strategy.

TIME NEEDED >
two or three days

SCIENCE >
psychology, anthropology

SCIENCE CONCEPTS >
visual memory, observation skills, perception, forming a hypothesis

ADULT INVOLVEMENT>
You'll need one or two teachers or other adult group leaders to help you with this experiment.

the **QUESTION >>** How do different people observe and remember the same situation?

the **PLAN >>** Stage a crime and study the variations in people's observations and responses to it. Then analyze what this information tells you about how detectives should proceed.

the buzz

In early 2007, 12-year-old Michael Auberry of Utah, on a Boy Scout camping trip in North Carolina, left the camp. He planned to go home because he was homesick. He intended to walk to a highway and hitchhike home, but he got lost in the unfamiliar woods. CNN reported that 25 search-and-rescue groups and several dog teams looked for Michael. After four days, a police officer with a search dog named Gandalf located Michael, who was cold and dehydrated but okay. He was more than a mile away from the camp. He had learned from the scouts to cover himself with leaves to stay warm.

the lingo

accomplice—someone who is working with you on something, usually a trick or crime

you'll need

a group of people
two accomplices—two teachers

NOTE: Two teachers and one class are ideal for this. You could try it at a large family gathering, but certain relatives might get annoyed!

what to do

1 **STAGE A CRIME** to occur in the midst of a group of people. With your accomplices, plan it precisely in advance so that you know where and when the crime will happen. Carefully note what you and your accomplices are wearing. Carefully plan and rehearse your actions so that you know exactly what to do.

2 **IMMEDIATELY AFTER THE CRIME IS COMMITTED,** have one accomplice come running in and tell everybody that the police need their assistance. The group must write down their observations in silence, being as detailed as possible about what they saw. Give each person a number and ask them to write their numbers on the paper.

3 **AFTER GATHERING THE OBSERVATIONS,** have the second accomplice talk to the class about what he or she saw. Then ask the group if they can now recall anything else about the crime. Ask them to write the new observations down with the same number they used before.

4 **ANALYZE YOUR RESULTS.** What do the two sets of observations have in common? What differences can you find between them?

5 **COMPARE THE OBSERVATIONS** with your plan and what you know about the staged crime. How many observers got the details, time, outfits, etc. right?

6 **WHAT WAS DIFFERENT** about the second set of observations?

7 **IMAGINE THAT YOU WERE** a police officer coming to the scene of this crime. What would the officer be looking for, based on the observations you gathered? How successful do you think he might be if he relied on these observations?

WORKSHOP RESOURCES >>

Build Your Memory.com: "Observation and Memory": http://www.buildyourmemory.com/observationandmemory.php

Police Magazine: http://www.policemag.com/

Search and Rescue Society of British Columbia: Behavior Characteristics of Lost People: http://www.sarbc.org/behchar.html

> Can you make generalizations about what males and females are more likely to observe, based on your data?

CONSIDER THIS! PRESENT THIS!

> Quote excerpts from the observations, show a photograph of the person who perpetrated your staged crime, and provide a graph showing the percentage of your observers who correctly observed different aspects of the crime and the criminal.

> **GO THE EXTRA MILE!** Is there more information you can get from your sample? Consider ways to categorize the observations the group made. For example, how many people recorded the time correctly? Who included information about colors, sizes, and other visual clues? Who included information about sounds? What other categories can you create?

NOW YOU SEE IT

(Assess how to improve visual memory)

TIME NEEDED >
one day

SCIENCE >
psychology, logic

SCIENCE CONCEPTS >
spatial relationships,
short-term memory,
visual memory

ADULT INVOLVEMENT>
None needed, but you
do need a partner to
help you.

the basics

ACCORDING TO PSYCHOLOGISTS, the ability to remember things short-term depends on three basic methods: recall, in which you memorize and then try to "call back" things to your mind; recognition, in which you pick something (or someone) from a lineup; and paired association, in which you link two things together in your mind, such as learning that "A" stands for "apple," which helps you to remember the sound "a" makes.

the buzz

Ohio State University researchers found that stress can help people memorize numbers. Stress causes the body to produce norepinephrine, also known as the "fight or flight" hormone. This hormone improves reactions in situations in which people feel threatened, such as when they're taking exams (as in the study) or at the scene of a crime. It also improves short-term memory, which is an emergency response.

the lingo

visual memory—memory of something you have observed

you'll need

photographs of a person
old magazines
scissors
glue stick
poster board
stopwatch, clock, or watch with a second hand

NOTE: *This is a great project to do with a partner.*

what to do

1 **CUT SMALL PICTURES** from a magazine. Cut out at least 130 different objects.

the QUESTION >> Can people be trained to be better witnesses by improving their short-term memory?

the PLAN >> Use a common test to find out how many pictures you can remember. Then train your visual memory and see if you can push your mental limits. Do this experiment on yourself or with a group of subjects.

2 **ASK SOMEONE TO PREPARE TEST SHEETS** for you by placing at least 12 pictures on a piece of poster board. The objects should be selected randomly. Determine ahead of time how you want them to be placed: in a row? in a random pattern? in no pattern? in boxes you draw ahead of time? Do not glue down the pictures. You'll need to use them again.

3 **HAVE YOUR PARTNER** show you the poster board with the objects and time you as you study it for 15 seconds.

4 **TRY TO RECALL THE 12 PICTURES YOU VIEWED.** How many can you list in 15 seconds?
• Repeat this test with another 12 objects and study them for a longer period of time—30 seconds,

45 seconds, or a minute.

- Repeat this test, but this time select the objects from another poster board in which the same pictures are shown among up to 100 other objects.
- Under which circumstances can you remember the most objects?

5 NEXT, DEVELOP METHODS FOR REMEMBERING MORE OBJECTS.

- Can you remember more objects if you alphabetize them in your head?
- Can you create a story in your head that includes the objects in order to remember them?
- Can you create a sentence or phrase that helps you remember the objects? For example, say the pictures show these objects:

shark, hummingbird, island, piano, microscope, egg, ostrich, ukulele, toilet, cheese, ankle, pencil. You might create the sentence "Ship me out, cap" (short for *captain*) in order to remember the objects.

- Can you remember the objects by noting their positions on the board?

6 FINALLY, SEE IF YOU CAN APPLY this concentration to remembering the details of a photograph of a person. In five seconds, observe the following:

- physical details
- size of the person (based on how high he sits or stands relative to, say, a light switch on the wall)
- clothing
- objects in the room
- other information you can gather from the photograph, such as time of day, location, etc.

CONSIDER THIS! PRESENT THIS!

> How are the skills involved in visual memory different from the observation skills explored in Workshop 7?

> Share your progress as you developed your memory. In your display, include the photograph you used in step #6. Ask visitors to study the photograph, then answer questions you prepared about the details within it. How do visitors account for their success in noticing and remembering the details?

WORKSHOP RESOURCES >>

You can use an online picture test to check your short-term memory. It's found at the University of Washington website: http://faculty.washington.edu/chudler/puzmatch.html

The Magic Mnemonic website has visuals that you might use instead of pictures: www.magicmnemonic.com

A great academic article about memory: http://www.healthline.com/galecontent/memory-1

ABOUT FACE

(How do people recognize faces?)

the basics

DETECTIVES USE MEASUREMENTS of the exact distances between your eyes, nose, ears, and the curves of your face. Later, they match your face with your measurements to identify you. They can identify people in face-front photographs in the same way.

TIME NEEDED >
a week or more

SCIENCE >
forensic anthropology, physiology, psychology

SCIENCE CONCEPTS >
face recognition, artificial intelligence

ADULT INVOLVEMENT>
You may need assistance and/or permission to test a number of subjects in face recognition.

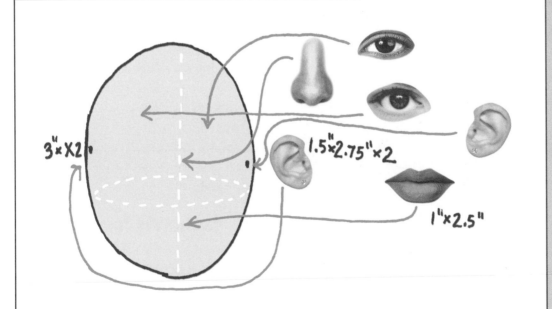

3"x2"

1.5"x2.75"x2

1"x2.5"

the buzz

What if a detective doesn't have a full view of the face he or she is trying to identify? Detectives use a computer program called Forensica to make the ID. Forensica is part of a biometrics package in the Amber Alert System, a plan that police use when children go missing and may have been kidnapped. "Say you have a two-dimensional photo of a person running away," says Paul Schuepp, who leads Animetrics, the company that created Forensica. "He's trying to hide his face, so we have only a partial 2-D view. We can create the rest of the face based on geometry and send out a video that shows the face as it turns back and forth, for easier identification."

the lingo

one-dimensional—linear, such as the edge of a sheet of paper; measured in length
two-dimensional—flat, such as the plane formed by a sheet of paper; measured in length and width
three-dimensional—contoured, such as a cube; measured in length, width, and height
avatar—a virtual (computer) model of a person that looks three-dimensional

you'll need

an assortment of faces of two types—people and dogs (see "Gathering Faces," below)
stopwatch
two sheets of foam core—one for people, one for dogs
index cards

gathering faces

Humans—Use magazines. Select a type of face based on features: eye

the QUESTION >> Is it easier for people to recognize people's faces or dogs' faces?

the PLAN >> Assemble two groups of faces with similar characteristics and compare people's proficiency at matching them.

color, skin color, and hair color and length. Find 20 people with similar features—for example, women with long brown hair, brown eyes, and light skin. Don't use famous people. (You want to work with identifying strangers, not people who might be recognized.)

Dogs—Choose one breed of dog, such as collies. Use dog magazines, or do an Internet image search for pictures of collies. Find 20 different collies with similar coloring.

what to do

1 **PRINT/CUT OUT YOUR PICTURES.** Make copies of your pictures, so that you have two sets. You may scan them into your computer, creating a slide for each, or paste the second set onto index cards.

2 **MAKE A POSTER.** For each group (people and dogs), attach the original set of pictures to each sheet of foam core. You'll have one poster showing all the people and one showing all the dogs.

3 **PLAN YOUR TEST.** Below are several ways to conduct the recognition test. You will test your subjects to see how long it takes them to find a face on the poster that matches the one on the card or

> " There is a **certain distance** between one *feature and another,* *a curvature,* **that says something** about, *say, what the* **mouth** **is going** *to look like.*
> "
>
> —Paul Schuepp, *Animetrics*

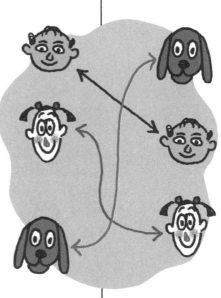

slide. You will compare the length of time it takes your subject to match dog faces and people faces. It's up to you which testing method you use, and whether you use just one testing method or compare several. Do what it takes to help you figure out what you want to know about how people recognize faces.

You might compare the methods, using several methods with the same group of subjects. Or you might choose just one method and then compare several groups or subjects by timing how long it takes them to recognize someone.

NOTE: *After the test is finished, ask subjects to reflect on what they went through. Which was harder to match, people or dogs? Why? Notice whether people's answers correlate with the category you tested first.*

RECOGNITION TEST METHODS

- Hide the poster of the people. Give the subject the stack of face cards. Reveal the poster and tell your subject to find the match among his cards. Repeat this process with the dog poster and cards. Time how long it takes for the subject to match his cards with each face on the posters.

- Hide the poster. Give the subject one face card to study. Decide on a length of time for study. (You may compare lengths of time as one experiment.) Take the face card away. Turn the poster over. Measure the length of time it takes for the subject to identify the face he studied.

- Instead of using a poster, make a matching set of cards. Have your subject study one card for a length of time you decide. Flip through the second set of cards one by one. Ask the subject to stop you when he spots the match to his card.

NOTE: *You will conduct each test, using the same method, with both people and dogs. Decide which group to do first for* all *your subjects.*

> Did your subjects match people's and dogs' faces at different rates? If so, what is your explanation?

CONSIDER THIS! PRESENT THIS!

> Include your posters and cards so that people visiting your exhibit can test themselves. Identify the matches that your subjects found most difficult to make, and display some of the dog or people faces that were most often chosen by mistake. Ask people who view your display to describe the differences among the similar faces. What kinds of words and descriptions do you hear most often?

> **GO THE EXTRA MILE!** Use metacognition, in which you ask your subjects to review their own performance and tell you about what types of learning they experienced. What went through their minds as they worked to make the matches? How well did they think they did at the task of matching people's and dogs' faces? What was easy? What were the difficulties? Did they get faster or more accurate as they went along? Was it easier or harder as the options decreased?

WORKSHOP RESOURCES >>

FaceResearch: http://www.faceresearch.org/

Face Recognition Home Page:
http://www.face-rec.org/general-info/

The Productive Aging Laboratory has a free database of photographs of faces.

PANTS ON FIRE

(Find the liar)

the basics

LIE DETECTION DEVICES (polygraph machines) are controversial in the intelligence and detective world because they may be wrong 10 to 30 percent of the time. But canny detectives do their best to use other clues, while spies and other criminals work to perfect their poker faces.

TIME NEEDED >
a weekend

SCIENCE >
psychology, physiology

SCIENCE CONCEPTS >
lie detection, physiology, psychology, body language, technology

ADULT INVOLVEMENT >
none

the buzz

Famous spy Aldrich Ames trained himself how NOT to be detected by a lie detector—and got away with spying on the U.S. for the Soviet Union. Ames worked for the Central Intelligence Agency (CIA), which is responsible for keeping other governments from spying on the U.S. Because he worked for the CIA he had access to the organization's sources and information. For nine years he used these resources to help Russia spy on the United States. In that time he gave away the identities of every U.S. operative in Russia. By the time Ames was caught, ten U.S. operatives had been killed by the Russian government.

the QUESTION >>

Can you learn how to read body language?

the PLAN >>

You'll devise, compare, and evaluate several different methods to determine whether someone is lying or telling the truth, using the way they speak, eye contact, the way they move, and the extent to which their expressions match what they're saying. Then you'll ask subjects to deliberately lie to you or tell the truth and assess your success at guessing which is which.

the lingo

body language—nonverbal communication

you'll need

about ten classmates
a video camera

what to do

1 **STUDY BEHAVIOR.** First, make a study of standard ways that psychologists say liars behave. See *Methods of Lie Detection* (next page) and *Resources* (p. 44).

2 **ASSEMBLE YOUR SUBJECTS.** About ten members of your class would work beautifully. Ask them to write three truths and a lie (four statements), and then to tell them all to you. You will try to guess which statement is the lie.

NOTE: Three Truths and a Lie *is a classic writing exercise in which writers learn to write the lie in the same manner as the truth in order to be as convincing as possible. The truths and lies may take the form of brief stories a sentence or more long (but no longer than a short paragraph).*

3 **ASSESS.** While you listen to each subject tell the stories, have someone film the subject. Then you can go back and review the video later to assess which one was the lie.

4 **FIRST IMPRESSIONS.** As you hear the story in person, jot down your first impressions. Is there a story you definitely think is true? Definitely a lie? Do your best to pay attention to HOW the person tells the story, not WHAT the story is about. What is it that makes you think the person is lying? Facial expression? Body movement? Gestures? Attitude?

5 **REVIEW** the videos separately. Study each person's movements, comparing the way they use their bodies during each story.

6 **OBSERVE.** Improve your chances of guessing whether someone is telling the truth or lying by asking questions of your subjects after they are finished telling their stories. Notice how they respond in words, facial expressions, and gestures.

7 **PREDICT.** Ask your subject which stories are true and which are lies. How often were you right? How often were you wrong? Did you get better at this or worse as you went along?

NOTE: *You may wish to divide your group. Hear one half's stories in person, then watch them on video and make your decisions. Get the answers and see how well you did, and study where you went wrong. Now do the activities with the second group to see if you improve.*

METHODS OF LIE DETECTION
Compare these to your videos and determine which are most useful and reliable as methods of lie detection.

- Someone who is lying will not touch his chest (where his heart lies).
- Someone who is lying will not make eye contact with the person he is lying to.
- When someone is telling a true story, he uses more hand gestures than he does when he is lying.
- When someone is telling a lie, he

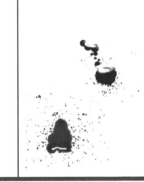

> ❝
>
> *93%* of our communication is nonverbal expression: the way we use our eyes and body movements.
>
> ❞
>
> —Janine Driver, *body language expert*

> What do you do when you're lying? Does lying change how you feel mentally and physically?

CONSIDER THIS! PRESENT THIS!

> For each behavior that you study as you try this activity, come up with a percentage effectiveness figure. For example, say you studied whether people say "uh" or "um" when they were lying. You found out that only four of your ten subjects did this. For this group, saying "um" or "uh" was only indicative of lying 40 percent of the time. Create a list of characteristics and their percentage rates for your display. Offer tips for lie detection. You may create a takeaway card for people visiting your science fair or invention convention booth.

> **GO THE EXTRA MILE!** If you like this study, look into ways people use body language when they're angry, frightened, or flirting.

may touch his face or mouth more often than when he is telling the truth.

- Smiles or frowns appear with a statement of happiness or sadness when someone is telling the truth. They may be out of sync when he is lying.
- Someone may use more words to tell a lie than he does to tell the truth.
- Using contractions (*can't*) is more common to truthtellers than liars (*cannot*).
- When lying, someone may say "uh" or "um" more often, may pause more often, and may speak more slowly.
- Liars blink less often.

WORKSHOP RESOURCES >>

How to Read Body Language: How to Tell If Someone Is Lying with Body Language:
http://www.youtube.com/watch?v=pXRQyJbMhkA

American Polygraph Association: www.polygraph.org

Changing Minds.org: http://changingminds.org/explanations/behaviors/body_language/body_language.htm

The Lie Behind the Lie Detector *by George W. Maschke and Gino J. Scalabrini:* www.antipolygraph.org/lie-behind-the-lie-detector.pdf

Learn more about Aldrich Ames and other spies at the FBI's Famous Cases file: http://www.fbi.gov/libref/historic/famcases/ames/ames.htm

FACING THE TRUTH

(Read split-second facial expressions)

the basics

DETECTIVES NEED TO BE ABLE TO "READ" FACES as they investigate a crime. Forty-three facial muscles are used to communicate emotions. Nineteenth-century researcher Guilliaume Duchenne first used photographs to study facial expressions. He noted that the muscles around the eyes are involved in the true smile but not in the phony one. So it's tough to fake a smile.

TIME NEEDED >
three or four days

SCIENCE >
psychology, physiology

SCIENCE CONCEPTS >
interpretation,
observation,
technology, behavior

ADULT INVOLVEMENT >
none

"Wait... wait... not yet... hold on..."

the buzz

Paul Ekman is working to understand why some detectives seem to have a sixth sense about liars. Ekman is a psychology professor at University of California Medical School, where he has learned that these detectives are more attuned than other people to microexpressions, or fleeting facial expressions. He is using what he has learned to advise the FBI and the CIA on how to read faces. With his program, called the Facial Action Coding System (FACS), Ekman can teach people to distinguish between truth and lies in under an hour.

NOTE: *FACS has been used by computer animators at the film studios Pixar and DreamWorks to give expressions to their characters, including Shrek and Buzz Lightyear.*

the QUESTION >> Can people distinguish between real and phony smiles?

the PLAN >> Conduct a study to see how many people successfully identify real and phony facial expressions. First, you'll prepare your video, which will show "actors" smiling real and fake smiles. Then you'll show the video to subjects and ask them to determine which smiles are real and which are fake.

the lingo

microexpressions—the small, quick movements of facial muscles that combine to form an expression. Some microexpressions are practically invisible to the naked eye, but when a film is shown in slow motion, they can be easily detected. Ekman thinks that most people perceive these microexpressions without realizing it.

you'll need

a video camera
a TV—to show your videos on
actors and subjects
a partner—to film while you interview your subjects

what to do

1 PREPARE YOUR VIDEO. Select three jokes. Try to find one that you think is hilarious, one you think is lame, and one that is somewhere in the middle. Film each actor separately. Say that you are going to tell them three jokes, and that you want them to smile at each one even if they don't think it's funny. Now tell the jokes in order while filming the actor's response. You may edit the jokes out of the videos and just show the responses, or show the whole thing.

2 SHOW YOUR VIDEO TO YOUR SUBJECTS. Ask them to keep score of real (R) and fake (F) smiles for each actor. The score sheet might look like this when filled in.

What's the story behind fake smiles? Why do people do this? Also, researchers have shown that the act of pretending to laugh activates some of the same feelings a real laugh creates. What chemicals are released when laughing? What is their function in your body?

CONSIDER THIS! PRESENT THIS!

Create a diagram of the face, labeling the different areas of the face that are used in a genuine smile and a fake smile. You may also use your videos at your display table.

GO THE EXTRA MILE! Here are two ways to expand your study: **1** Slowing down a video may reveal microexpressions not easily noticed at regular speed. **2** Researchers trying to get better at reading faces sometimes watch TV with the sound off. Compare results with and without sound.

WORKSHOP RESOURCE >>
The BBC Science website asks you to distinguish fake and real smiles: http://www.bbc.co.uk/science/humanbody/mind/surveys/smiles/index.shtml

SCORE SHEET

	A1	A2	A3
KNOCK KNOCK	R	F	F
DOG says "Hi"	R	R	F
Macaroni	F	F	F

NOT BY THE HAIR OF MY CHINNY CHIN CHIN!

(Study hair)

TIME NEEDED >
one weekend

SCIENCE >
forensics, genetics

SCIENCE CONCEPT >
DNA

ADULT INVOLVEMENT >
none

the basics

A **DETECTIVE TRYING TO IDENTIFY** the origin of a hair found at a crime scene studies hair diameter, the medulla, the number and distribution of color (or pigment) granules, and the level of color and coarseness.

the buzz

In 2005, DNA analysis was used to prove that hair found near Edmonton, Canada, which eyewitnesses declared to belong to the legendary Sasquatch, actually belonged to a bison. The witnesses found the hair stuck on a bush where they had reportedly seen a hairy, apelike monster, the sort frequently associated with Bigfoot. (See also Workshop 3)

the lingo

medulla—the central core or marrow of a shaft of hair

color granules—hair, like skin, gets its color from a substance called melanin. Melanin granules give the hair its color, and the fairer the hair is, the fewer granules of melanin it has.

coarseness—the level of smoothness hair has

you'll need

two microscope slides for each person (total 20)
a dissecting microscope
wax pencil or small removable stickers
two hairs from the heads of ten different people—Consider gathering one hair found in a comb and one pulled from the subject's head (ask the subject to do it herself). This will allow you to compare hair that has dropped out naturally with hair that has been pulled out of the head, a useful clue in forensics.
pencil and paper—to draw samples
still camera/microscope—to photograph samples
eyedropper (optional)

the QUESTION >> What can you learn from studying a hair?

the PLAN >> Examine hairs to learn about different aspects of their makeup and try to match them with a small number of subjects.

NOTE: *Taking still photographs through a microscope requires a special camera adapter. These cost around $100! Find out if your school has one, or see if you can use one from a local high school or university. (They might let you visit and use their microscope; just bring your own slides.) See* Resources *for a source for your own camera adapter.*

TWO METHODS FOR EXAMINING HAIR:

1. Dry mount slide—Place a hair on a slide and cover it with a cover slip.

2. Wet mount slide—Place a hair on a slide, use an eyedropper to drop one drop of water on it, and

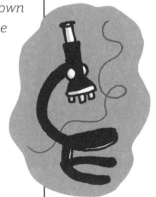

set the cover slip gently on top. The idea here is to use the water as a cushion, so the amount of water you use should be just enough to rest the cover slip on top. The water should not bubble out of the sides. This can be tricky because sometimes you don't have enough water. You can fix this without taking the cover slip off. Just drip a little water next to the edge of the cover slip; the extra water should seep under it to make the cushion you need.

Draw conclusions: how useful would a microscope be in analyzing hair found at the scene of a crime? Could hair help lead a detective to a suspect or give other clues?

CONSIDER THIS! PRESENT THIS!

Include images of hair in photographs or artwork and comparisons of features of hair at magnification.

GO THE EXTRA MILE! You might make a scale for a hair characteristic, such as coarseness, assigning a number from 1 to 5, where 1 is the smoothest and 5 is the coarsest.

NOTE: *One reason detectives search for hair is that it doesn't break down (decompose) easily, even when on the head of a dead person. Long after a crime, when body fluids have disappeared, hair can still be found and used as evidence in understanding what happened at a crime scene.*

what to do

1 **GATHER HAIR** and assemble your slides. Use a wax pencil or small removable sticker to identify each slide.

2 **VIEW HAIR** through a microscope and then either draw each sample or photograph it with a still camera through the microscope.

3 **COMPARE.** Compare and contrast the hairs. Note the differences and make inferences about how features observed at magnification—such as cortex, color granules, and coarseness—relate to the appearance, color, and texture of the hair.

4 **MATCH.** Match two hairs from each subject. Can you do this through observation alone?

WORKSHOP RESOURCE >>

The Human Genome Project website has pages about forensic identification: http://www.ornl.gov/sci/techresources/Human_Genome/elsi/forensics.shtml

BLOOD ON YOUR HANDS

(Analyze spilled blood)

the basics

DIFFERENT INJURIES WILL CAUSE BLOOD to show up in different patterns and quantities. In general, drops of a liquid try to stay spherical. Blood drips straight down onto a surface and tends to form a circular spatter; but if it falls at an angle, the drop may be an oval or drawn out into the shape of a streak with a tail that shows the direction it fell.

TIME NEEDED >
a weekend

SCIENCE >
physics, fluid dynamics

SCIENCE CONCEPT >
serology (the study of blood)

ADULT INVOLVEMENT >
assistance in the kitchen and using the drill

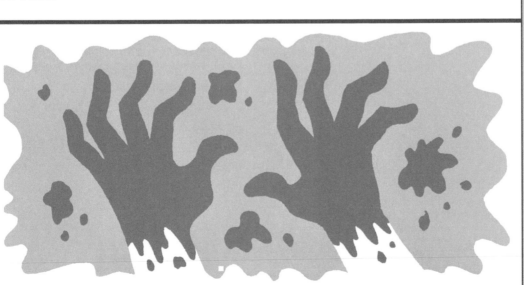

spherical because forces on them are equal. But at the surface, molecules hold on to each other more tightly because the forces on them are unequal.

the buzz

Among other tasks, forensic serologists examine the patterns in blood found at a crime scene for evidence of the activity that took place there.

the lingo

serology—the study of blood
surface tension—molecules in the interior part of a liquid tend to be

you'll need

PVC piping, 6 feet
piece of wood—2 x 4 x 12 inches
dowel—1/4 to 1/2 inch in diameter and long enough to pass through the two sides of your PVC pipe and extend about six inches out from one side
screws and a screwdriver
drill and drill bit large enough for the diameter of your dowel
a spring—about 1/2 inch in diameter (to fit around the dowel) and about 2 inches long
gardening wire
plastic syringe—available at pharmacies or farm supply stores (no needle included)
flooring samples—tile, carpet, vinyl, wood, stone, concrete
baby food jar—for holding blood
fake blood—you can buy stage blood at a costume store or make your own from the below recipe

RECIPE FOR FAKE BLOOD:
Experiment to find the combination of these ingredients that most closely resembles the appearance and consistency of blood:
    1/2 cup smooth peanut butter

the QUESTION >> Gravity, physics, properties of liquids: can understanding how the world works help you understand the clues you observe?

the PLAN >> Experiment with blood spatter patterns from different heights and angles and onto different surfaces.

TRANSFER	TRANSFER	PASSIVE	PASSIVE	ARTERIAL SPURT

Blood spatter analysis is one way that blood at a crime scene gives information about who was there and what happened.

about 1/2 cup cooking oil
1—2 teaspoons red food coloring

what to do

Research and complete this list of questions and calculations.

1 SET UP YOUR SPATTERER.

A. Measure 18 inches from one end of the pipe. At that point, drill straight through the pipe to make a pair of holes for the dowel to pass through. Continue to drill through the pipe every two inches until you get to the other end.

B. Secure the undrilled end of the pipe to the block of wood, using screws.

C. Wire the spring to one end of the dowel, and attach the spring to the push-in end of the syringe.

D. Your finished spatterer will allow you to experiment with the dowel

by positioning it at different heights from the floor.

2 MEASURE. Mark and measure the distance from the floor to the syringe tip when it is positioned at different holes on the PVC pipe. Number the holes if you find that helpful.

3 EXPERIMENT AND RECORD. Move the dowel

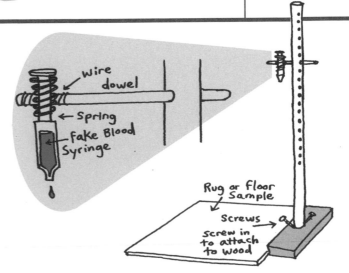

> " *Whether a* **video camera** *is available or not, it is* **absolutely essential** *that* **still photographs** *are taken to* **document the crime scene** *and any associated* **blood** *evidence.* "

—George Schiro, forensic scientist,
"Bloodstain Photography," Louisiana State Police Crime Laboratory

into the first set of holes and fill the syringe with the blood. Carefully and precisely record the angle of the syringe then fire it. Repeat at each height. For each firing of the syringe, be sure to control all the variables: fill the syringe to the same level and match the temperature and ventilation level of the room for each test (for example, if you did the first test with the door closed, keep the door closed for each firing to prevent breezes from changing the outcome). Position different floorings under your device for a more diverse experiment.

NOTE: *Precise measurement and replication is one criterion for a good scientific experiment because it allows for other scientists to repeat experiments and get the same results.*

4 **COMPARE** the spatter patterns of different floorings, different heights, and different angles as you learn what happens as you fire the syringe full of blood.

WORKSHOP RESOURCE >>

A tutorial in analyzing blood spatters is available:
http://www.bloodspatter.com/BPATutorial.htm

What other information could a detective gather from blood clues?

CONSIDER THIS! PRESENT THIS!

George Schiro reports that photographs of blood spatters can be used to re-create the scene of a crime long after all evidence has been removed. The spatter can be isolated with Adobe Photoshop and made into a PowerPoint slide. The slide can then be projected with an LCD projector onto the wall or floor to show exactly how the scene looked right after the crime.

GO THE EXTRA MILE! Photograph and/or video your procedure and the resulting spatters.

CRIMINALS USE TRICKS

(Deflect people's attention with sleight of hand)

the basics

SLEIGHT OF HAND IS THE KEY to many magic tricks, stage combat, and other theatrics. By learning to use prestidigitation and other tricks of the trade, understanding how people respond to them, and assessing what bystanders will notice, you can become a better detective.

TIME NEEDED >
a week, a month, or a year

SCIENCE >
psychology, behavior

SCIENCE CONCEPTS >
observation, perception

ADULT INVOLVEMENT >
none

the buzz

Often criminals work in teams; while one creates a diversion, the other commits a crime. For example, a scuffle at the bottom of an escalator can distract people on the escalator so that they don't notice that a pickpocket is riding along with them and making their pockets lighter. Magicians hold conventions to compare notes on their methods of prestidigitation, while on the streets illegal "shell games" are used to scam passersby who think they can outwit the gamesters. By learning about how diversions are created, you can become sharper at understanding crimes.

QUESTION >> Can you deflect people's attention from something happening right in front of their eyes?

PLAN >> Learn to play the classic shell game honestly and dishonestly, and compare the responses of your audience.

the lingo

prestidigitation—sleight of hand; literally, the word means "fast fingers"

palm—to pick up a small object in your hand, such as a pea, without anyone seeing it there

load—to put down an object—for instance, to put the pea under a shell without anyone seeing you do it

you'll need

three "shells"—classically these are seashells or coconut shells, but they can be bottle caps, jar lids, or boxes turned upside down

three "peas"—classically these are dried peas, but they can be stones, marbles, or other small three-dimensional objects

players—to play the shell game

what to do

1 **HONEST VERSION.** Hide the pea under one shell, switch the shells around, and ask your player to pick the shell where the pea is hidden. Play ten times with each player in order to figure out how likely the player is to guess the location of the pea. How can you best fool the player? How can the player get better at guessing? You can decide for yourself how many players to play with in order to assemble

your data about ways to improve wins and losses for the shell man (you) and the player.

2 **DISHONEST VERSION.** Learn to "palm" and "load" the pea in order to remove it and replace it while fooling the player into thinking he knows where it is.

A. Practice picking up a pea in the fold between the center of your palm and the fleshy base of your thumb, keeping your hand relaxed and your eyes focused elsewhere. Practice in the mirror, or have a friend take a video of you so you can see your mistakes. Once you perfect this with one hand, learn to do it with the other. Then learn to do something different with the free hand to divert attention from the one that's palming the pea.

B. Practice moving the pea in your palm without making it obvious that you have something in your hand. Keep your hand in a relaxed, open position.

C. Practice loading the pea under a shell while seeming to simply move the shell around. Distract the player's attention with your other hand.

D. Practice your poker face.

NOTE: *This is the long part of this workshop. The more you practice, the better step 3 will be.*

3 **NOW PLAY** ten times with a player. What do you notice? Play with the same number of players you used in part one. How do the honest version and dishonest version compare?

WORKSHOP RESOURCES >>

Ricky Jay is considered the greatest sleight-of-hand man in the world. His website is: http://rickyjay.com

Magicians Penn and Teller demonstrate sleight of hand in video (using a cigarette, among other objects): www.youtube.com/watch?v=_qQX-jayixQ

> How can you use a partner to help you learn whether the player trusts you or not? Does the player's response change if she is losing or winning?

CONSIDER THIS! PRESENT THIS!

> Make your shell game the center of your presentation. Ask observers to vote on which shell the pea is under at certain points. How many people think you're cheating after watching you go through a few turns of the shell?

> GO THE EXTRA MILE! Combine this activity with the observation test in Workshop 7 by staging a crime that involves prestidigitation or a diversion created by an accomplice. What effect does the diversion or sleight of hand have on the observations and memories of your observers?

THE WRITER DID IT

(Analyze handwriting and paper fibers)

TIME NEEDED >
one day

SCIENCE >
physiology, psychology, forensic graphology

SCIENCE CONCEPTS >
pattern analysis, comparison, observation, fibers, behavior

ADULT INVOLVEMENT >
none

the basics

HANDWRITING IS CONSIDERED too difficult to fake, and for this reason it is used to determine whether the same person wrote two samples: a piece of evidence (such as a check written against an account that doesn't belong to the person) and a sample taken from a suspect. But studies have shown that handwriting isn't a good indicator of what someone's personality is like. So, besides helping identify someone, handwriting analysis has its limits in detective work.

the buzz

In 1993, the U.S. Supreme Court determined that handwriting was not reliable evidence that someone had committed a crime. Handwriting analysts only had a 52 percent accuracy rate at that time. But in 2002, a computer programmed to match samples was correct 96 percent of the time. So detectives still use handwriting samples, as well as the paper they're written on, as clues from the scene of a crime. They can often be matched with notebooks found among a suspect's possessions.

the lingo

evidence—a clue that can be used to confirm or deny a suspect's guilt

you'll need

test group—a teacher and class that are not your own; choose a class in which you know few people. If you know the handwriting of anyone in that classroom, exclude them from your test group.
notepads—a batch of small notepads or old notebooks with a few blank pages
a box of pens that are all the same
magnifying lens
dissecting microscope
camera or cell phone (optional)

what to do

1 **CHOOSE A PARAGRAPH** from a book that you would like to have your test group write for the sample. Give it to the teacher of the class, and ask him or her to have each student copy the paragraph twice: once on a sheet of paper to be left in the pad or notebook, and once on a sheet to be ripped out.

the QUESTION >> Can you match clues to suspects by means of their handwriting or paper?

the PLAN >> Gather handwriting and paper samples from a group of people whose handwriting you do not know. Use handwriting and paper analysis to try to match them.

2 **ALL SAMPLES AND SOURCES SHOULD BE NUMBERED** by the teacher in a random way so that there is no logical connection between them. The teacher should keep track of which samples and sources (pads or notebooks) go together for later use in assessing how well you match them.

3 **THE STUDENTS SHOULD TEAR** the ripped-out sheets of paper exactly in half. All notebooks and pads and halves of the loose sheets should come to you for analysis.

4 **TRY TO MATCH TORN SAMPLES** to each other and then to the pad or notebook source. Try all of the following methods:
a. visual identification of handwriting matches
b. magnified and microscope identification of handwriting matches
c. visual identification of paper matches
d. magnified and microscope identification of paper matches
e. visual identification of torn edge matches
f. magnified and microscope identification of torn edge matches

5 **AFTER YOU HAVE ASSESSED ALL OF THE MATCHES,** compare the results with the teacher's master list. How well did you do at matching?

WORKSHOP RESOURCES >>

American Handwriting Analysis Foundation:
http://www.handwritingfoundation.org/

Forensic Biology website on graphology:
http://www.bxscience.edu/publications/forensics/articles/document/r-hand01.htm

News about graphology and its uses:
The Forgery Detective: http://theforgerydetective.com

CONSIDER THIS! PRESENT THIS!

> How effective do you think your methods are for providing reliable evidence? Could your method be used fairly to prove that a suspect is guilty?

> Photograph your magnified samples through the microscope lens. It's especially easy to do this with a cell phone camera, because the lens is usually flush with the flat surface of the phone, so it can be easily positioned over the microscope eyepiece. Transfer the photographs to your computer and print them for use in your project display.

> GO THE EXTRA MILE! Study whether paper ripped by a right-handed person looks different from paper ripped by a left-handed person.

READING THE MAIL

(Decipher the postal bar code)

the basics

COULD YOUR MAILBOX BE A CRIME SCENE? Bar codes are one way that the U.S. Postal Service streamlines mail delivery and keeps mail out of the wrong hands. A letter that comes without a bar code or canceled stamp might not have been processed by the U.S. Postal Service, and it might indicate that something's fishy.

TIME NEEDED >
one day

SCIENCE >
mathematics, physics

SCIENCE CONCEPTS >
coding, analyzing,
ultraviolet light, logic

ADULT INVOLVEMENT >
none

the buzz

Pitney Bowes is a company that creates mechanisms, methods, and systems to protect the mail from crimes such as the anthrax scares of 2002, pipe bombs, and hate mail. Douglas Quine of Pitney Bowes provided the bar code information for this workshop.

the QUESTION >> Can you decode a bar code the way the U.S. Postal Service does?

the PLAN >> Analyze and try out the methods that the U.S. Postal Service uses to encode the mail.

the lingo

bar code—a code that uses a system of printed bars of different lengths to represent numbers

you'll need

**several different pieces of mail
a black-lightbulb (ultraviolet lightbulb) and light source**

what to do

Analyze the bar code on a letter to see whether the machine read the address correctly.

How to read the bar code on your letter:

1 Most U.S. letter bar codes have bars of two lengths: long and short.

2 Every bar code should start and end with long bars; ignore those.

3 Look at the rest of the bars in groups of five, starting with the second bar. Each group of five bars represents one digit. Here's how to figure out what those digits are.

The five bars stand for one of these numbers: 7, 4, 2, 1, 0.

Some genius figured out that this range would allow you to come up with the digits 0 to 9. You do it by adding the numbers of the long bars together.

Say you have this bar code:

    ‖‖‖
    74210

Here, the 4 and 2 places have long bars.

Added together, they total 6, so this bar code stands for 6.

Say you have this barcode:

    ‖‖
    74210

The 1 and 0 places have long bars.

Added together, they total 1, so this bar code stands for 1.

Say you have this: ‖|‖‖‖ 74210

The 7 and 4 places have long bars. Added together, they total 11, but there is no 11 in this system, so this bar code stands for 0.

Now let's look at the bar code on a letter.

after the house or box number. This is called a checksum. Add it to all of the other digits in the bar code, and the sum should be a multiple of 10. If it doesn't add up, this shows something's wrong or missing in the bar code. Additional numbers may be included to indicate that the mail requires special services, such as a registered or certified piece of mail that needs a special signature.

WORKSHOP RESOURCE >>

Doug Quine's barcode decoder:
http://www.triskelion-ltd.com/postnetj.html

0 6 8 0 1 0 1 5 3 3 2

Ignore the first and last bars of the whole bar code. Then look at the next 25 bars to find the zip code: 06801.

The next two sets of five bars give your mail route. The mail route is #1.

The next two sets of five bars are your mail carrier's number. The mail carrier is #53.

The rest of the bars in the bar code indicate the house or mailbox number. The house number is 32.

NOTE: *Many bar codes include an extra set of five bars at the end,*

Use your black light to study money. Which bills fluoresce?

CONSIDER THIS! PRESENT THIS!

Scan, enlarge, and print out the mail you analyzed, and create labels that indicate the different features that you analyzed.

GO THE EXTRA MILE! Stamps with one value do not fluoresce. Why do you think the U.S. Postal Service does not include fluorescence in this stamp? Use your black light to scan stamps of different values.

BIOWARFARE DEFENSE

(Study and compare anthraxlike substances)

TIME NEEDED >
one or two days

SCIENCE >
microbiology, physics,
aerodynamics

SCIENCE CONCEPTS >
buoyancy, aerophysics

ADULT INVOLVEMENT >
none

the basics

ANTHRAX IS A DISEASE spread by the bacterium *Bacilla anthracis*, a powdery, practically weightless, nearly invisible material. These bacteria can stay alive for a long time. If you inhale the anthrax spores, they can settle in your lungs and cause pneumonia.

the buzz

Could individuals or communities be attacked with diseases? Yes. That's exactly what happened during the anthrax scares of the early 2000s, when several people became seriously ill or died as a result of anthrax sent through the mail.

the lingo

biological warfare—using germs as weapons

you'll need

sticky clear paper—shelf liner or contact paper
construction paper—dark shade (red and black are best)
a variety of powders—confectioners' sugar, granulated sugar, baby powder, sand
water—in containers with metric markings
stopwatch—or a clock or watch with a second hand
video camera—(optional)

the QUESTION >>

Can you use kitchen equipment to identify some of the properties of powders that behave similarly to anthrax, in order to consider ways to prevent poisons from coming into contact with people?

the PLAN >>

Conduct three experiments to understand more about how anthrax might be dispersed through the mail.

what to do

Anthrax Experiment #1:
Powder on the Floor

1 **CUT** a one-foot-square piece of contact paper for each different powder you try. Remove the backing from the sticky paper and place it on the floor, sticky side up. Weight it to keep it still.

2 **DROP** small amounts of different powders from different heights. Record how much powder you drop and the height from which you drop it.

3 **COVER** your contact paper with the construction paper, being careful to smooth out the wrinkles. When you turn it over you will see your powder pattern clearly

against the dark paper.

Be sure to note if there were conditions that moved the air in the room you experimented in. How did the movement of the air affect your powder drop?

Anthrax Experiment #2: *Powder in the Envelope*

Anthrax is tiny and light. It can seep out of the corners and edges of envelopes, giving the lie to the theory that as long as you don't open the mail, you're safe from anthrax poisoning.

Try to seal powder into an envelope.

1 **TRY DIFFERENT WAYS** of encasing powder in an envelope: fold it into paper first, pour it directly into the envelope, or seal it inside a plastic bag before putting it in the envelope.

2 **SEAL THE ENVELOPE** as you normally would. Also experiment with different ways of sealing: using a wet sponge, licking, or taping.

3 **CARRY THE ENVELOPE** in your hand across a path of dark construction paper or a rug. Notice whether you see powder emerging, falling, and/or landing on the rug or paper.

4 **SHAKE THE ENVELOPE** as though you were trying to see through it or trying to make the powder come out. Does more emerge than before?

5 **USE YOUR OBSERVATIONS** to make some predictions about how a material as light as anthrax might behave inside an envelope.

WORKSHOP RESOURCE >>
Center for Disease Control website about anthrax: http://www.cdc.gov/ncidod/dbmd/diseaseinfo/anthrax_g.htm

CONSIDER THIS! PRESENT THIS!

How would you stop the spread of anthrax, knowing what you've learned about how powder travels?

Show the rate at which the powder traveled, in the air and from a sealed envelope. Suggest the ways you've thought of to clean up a potential anthrax event. Take into consideration the natural air movements of inside and outside environments.

GO THE EXTRA MILE! Set up a station where visitors may experiment with powders of different sizes and weights to see how they fall or how they behave when you try to seal them into an envelope.

DNA NECKLACE

(Extract your own DNA)

the basics

DNA STANDS FOR DIOXYRIBONUCLEIC (de-oxee-ry-bo-nu-clay-ick) acid. DNA is a protein, a substance formed by chains of paired amino acids. The pairs form in patterns called a sequence. This sequence is different for every individual organism, plant or animal. Your DNA is found in every cell in your body, and it can be used to identify you.

TIME NEEDED >
a day

SCIENCE >
microbiology, genetics

SCIENCE CONCEPTS >
DNA as evidence, the human genome

ADULT INVOLVEMENT >
needed for lab procedures

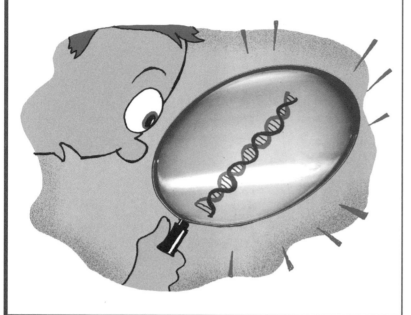

the QUESTION >> What does DNA look like?

the PLAN >> Extract DNA from the cells of the skin inside your cheek.

the buzz

Eleven-year-old Brian Shields of Northport, New York, gave me this idea. He went to DNA camp at Cold Spring Harbor Laboratory. Brian came home with a piece of his own DNA in a special little capsule on a string around his neck. What does DNA have to do with crime scenes? Plenty. Since hair, blood, and other body substances contain DNA, DNA extraction has become a vital clue in identifying criminals.

the lingo

incubate—to provide the conditions under which a living thing can grow and develop

you'll need

bottled beverage—sports drink or other clear, colored drink (such as cranberry juice)
95% ethanol (ethyl alcohol)
1.5-milliliter tube—with a hinged cap (see *Resources* for suppliers)
string
graduated cylinder—with milliliter (ml) markings along the side
test tube
paper cup
timer or watch with second hand
eye dropper
soap solution—Cold Spring Harbor Laboratory experimented to find the best mix. They recommend combining 20 ml of shampoo with 60 ml of distilled water.

what to do

1 **MEASURE** six ml of sports drink and pour it into the paper cup. Save the rest to drink later; you won't need it for this experiment.

2 **SWISH** all six ml of the sports drink in your mouth for 30 seconds.

3 **SPIT** the liquid back into the paper cup. Now your cells (from your saliva and the inside of your mouth) are dissolved in the sports drink. It's a cell solution.

4 **POUR** the cell solution into the test tube.

5 **POUR** two ml of soap solution into the cell solution. The total of the solution will now be eight ml.

6 **GENTLY** swirl the test tube to mix it.

7 **INCUBATE** the solution by leaving it to sit at room temperature for two minutes.

8 **HOLD** the test tube at an angle. Use an eye dropper to carefully add three ml of ethanol to the top of the solution in the tube. The idea is to let the ethanol form a layer on top of the soap solution.

9 **SET** the test tube down. Wait two minutes. You should see DNA floating in the ethanol. It will look like small dots or strands.

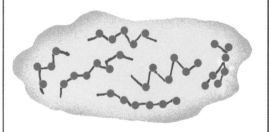

WORKSHOP RESOURCES >>

This activity is used courtesy of the DNA Lab Camp at Cold Spring Harbor Laboratory, Dolan DNA Learning Center: http://www.dnalc.org/home.html

Get 1.5-ml capped tubes and other supplies from USA Scientific: www.usascientific.com

How to Extract DNA from Anything Living: http://learn.genetics.utah.edu/content/labs/extraction/howto/

> How can one person's DNA be distinguished from another's? Use the Internet to learn more.

CONSIDER THIS! PRESENT THIS!

> Create a Web page showing what you did.

> **GO THE EXTRA MILE!** Use the eye dropper to transfer 1 ml of the ethanol to the 1.5-ml tube. Close an 18-inch length of string into the hinge, and then close the cap. Knot the string around your neck to make a necklace of a test tube of your own DNA.

WHO DIED?

(Take attendance at a decomposition)

TIME NEEDED >
two weeks

SCIENCE >
forensic entomology,
microbiology

SCIENCE CONCEPTS >
decomposition, decay,
organic materials,
bacteria, insects, and
other corpse fauna

ADULT INVOLVEMENT>
permission to let
something get rancid
and insect-ridden;
permission to use a
dissecting microscope
from a school or
laboratory

the basics

THE AGE OF A CORPSE—how long it's been dead—is measured by the age and stage of bacteria and bugs growing on and in the body. If you can come up with a time line of what typically happens as flesh decomposes, then when you observe something happening in an organism that has died, you can tell how long it's been dead—and pinpoint the time of death.

the buzz

At the University of Tennessee Medical Center, the FBI maintains a field of cadavers (dead human bodies) called the Body Farm as a decomposition laboratory. Their research helps them to solve crimes.

the lingo

forensic entomology—the study of insects that colonize dead bodies to figure out the time of death
corpse—a cadaver or dead body
fauna—animals

you'll need

food samples from the four food groups—raw meat or fish, vegetables or fruit, bread, and cheese
magnifying lens
dissecting microscope
bug identification guides
open-air area—such as a rooftop, wall, or compost bin that is open to let in bugs but not birds or animals
storage containers—recyclable plastic with lids
camera or video camera (optional)

NOTE: *While you wait for your foods to become bug-infested, set up the video camera with your microscope in order to film the results of your experiment (see instructions at right).*

the QUESTION >> What lives and lays eggs on something dead or dying?

the PLAN >> Observe, compare, and analyze what colonizes a decomposing body.

HOW TO **ADAPT** A MICROSCOPE TO A VIDEO CAMERA

YOU'LL NEED—a dissecting microscope, video camera, masking tape

WHAT TO DO

1. If the microscope belongs to your school, ask the teacher to schedule time for you, and get permission to remove the eyepiece of the microscope.
2. There are two lenses on the eyepiece tube of the scope. The one at the top is the eye lens, and the one at the bottom is the ocular lens. Unscrew the eye lens (the top one) and set it aside.
3. Now turn the lens over so that the ocular lens is on top. Take a strip of masking tape and wrap it around the eyepiece tube. Important: usually the eye lens holds the eyepiece up. Without it, the eyepiece could slide into the tube. The tape will keep it snug. Now push the eyepiece back into the scope. The ocular lens is now on top.
4. Use a tripod to position your video camera over the microscope, aiming it to get a clear image.

Suggested by Dr. Shawn Carlson of Labrats and the Society of Amateur Scientists.

what to do

1 **SET UP FOUR STORAGE CONTAINERS.** Place a small sample of uncooked food inside each. Leave the lids off.

2 **KEEP A CAREFUL RECORD** of what you observe through your senses for the next several days. Record the temperature in the area where your samples are. Note whether you can see signs that bugs or other creatures have been attracted to your samples. You may want to photograph the samples each day.

3 **DETERMINE INTERVALS** at which you will remove the samples from the container to examine them, perhaps on the second, fourth, sixth, and eighth days.

4 **AT EACH INTERVAL,** remove a piece of each sample and examine it with the magnifying lens and microscope. Count, identify, and sketch the bugs that colonize each sample. Add descriptions to your journal, as well as your sensory observations: texture, color, and smell. (NOTE: Don't taste!) Draw, video, microscope-video, or photograph the samples.

WORKSHOP RESOURCES >>

National Geographic Body Farm video: http://video. nationalgeographic.com/video/player/science/health- human-body-sci/human-body/body-farm-sci.html

The Australian Museum website Death On Line describes the stages of decomposition of a body, and lists corpse fauna—the bacteria and bugs associated with it—in its page "Decomposition: What happens to the body after death?" The site includes time-elapse photography of the decomposition of a piglet.
http://www.deathonline.net/decomposition/

How Stuff Works: Body Farm:
http://science.howstuffworks.com/body-farm.htm

> How long do you think it would take for your food sample to disappear completely?

CONSIDER THIS! PRESENT THIS!

> Include a time line created for each food sample, based on your observations and a graph comparing how your samples changed and decomposed over time.

PICTURE THIS

(Heighten observation and memory)

the basics

DR. HENRY LEE DESCRIBES BEING A DETECTIVE as reconstructing events—creating a step-by-step sequence of what happened based on observation and physical evidence. Lee has been very successful in helping to solve criminal mysteries because he thinks "outside of the box," considering clues that others might overlook. Photographs are often his most important tool at the scene of a crime.

TIME NEEDED >
one day

SCIENCE >
scientific method and procedure

SCIENCE CONCEPTS >
forensic photography, observation, interpretation, extrapolation

ADULT INVOLVEMENT >
Consult a parent or guardian before interviewing potential witnesses who are strangers, and before asking for input from experts.

the buzz

Some soldiers in the Iraq war were specially trained as forensic photographers who took pictures at the scenes of suicide bombings and other incidents. After the fact, their photographs helped intelligence personnel learn the identities of suicide bombers and the circumstances behind their activities.

the QUESTION >> How does photography help detectives observe and analyze a crime scene?

the PLAN >> Explore evidence to unearth a story—if not a crime—in your house or neighborhhood. The key here is to identify the scene where an event took place. You'll gather evidence through observation and record it in words, drawings, and photographs; interview people who might have more information; and draw conclusions that allow you to tell the story.

the lingo

intelligence—secret information or activities conducted by a government or other institution

you'll need

35 mm camera
sketchpad and/or notebook
optional: recording device, tripod

what to do

1 **BE ON THE LOOKOUT FOR STORIES.** What you're looking for is evidence that something happened here. Consider the story (not necessarily a crime) evidenced by these:

- a small pile of peanut shells, soda cans, and pencil shavings in front of a convenience store. (How many people? What were they doing? How long were they here?)
- a dead chipmunk outside the back door (Was it a cat? Whose cat? Which cat? Was it a hungry cat? A playful cat? Or was it something else besides a cat? Where and when was the chipmunk caught?)
- a trail of milk droplets and a few Lucky Charms leading up the stairs from the kitchen (Whodunnit? How can you prove it?)
- a faded, broken lobster claw—bound with an intact rubber band—is lying on the beach (Who

banded the lobster? Where were they when it happened? What happened after that?)

2 **BEFORE MOVING ANYTHING,** photograph the evidence. Photography comes first before anything is moved.

3 **MAKE A SKETCH** in order to help you remember the exact positions of things. Include any notes you have about items in the scene.

4 **WRITE** a description of the scene. Include factors that might not show up in your photographs or sketch, such as temperature, weather now and in the recent past, and other information that you have about the case (such as the fact that you observed the cat lurking in the grass under the tree before finding the dead chipmunk).

5 **DON'T NEGLECT** to search the area for other clues. Is there a peanut bag—or a crumpled drawing or letter—in the trash in front of the convenience store?

Is there fur or blood in the grass? Is there an empty bowl in your brother's room?

6 **INTERVIEW** possible witnesses or experts.

WORKSHOP RESOURCE >>

Dr. Henry Lee's website:
http://www.drhenrylee.com/famous/

Share your conclusions in the form of a narrative—a step-by-step sequence of events that answers the questions who, what, where, when, and how—if not why.

CONSIDER THIS! PRESENT THIS!

Make a sketch of the scene of a crime, keying it to your photos so you can show where your closeups fit in the big picture. Arrange your photos in order of discovery. Include transcripts or recordings of your witness testimonies.

GO THE **EXTRA** MILE! Share your story with an expert (such as a local police officer or news reporter) and get advice and new insight.

PRESENT IT!

HANDING IT IN, SHOWING IT OFF, telling your story, getting that "A." It all comes down to strong science and strong communication. Your presentation tells the story of your work. Tell it well with clear language, visuals, and a little drama.

INCLUDE IT! Your starting question(s), procedures, tools, data (facts), findings (results), notes, conclusion (decision based on the facts and results), and a follow-up question. Provide a listing of your research: articles, books, websites, interviews, and other sources you used.

DRAW IT! You're working with changeable conditions—fluids and soil that may dry out, impressions that may be rubbed out, prints that may fade. Photograph things first, and then create sketches and maps that help you preserve and understand the relationships between things—how far apart things are and at what angle to one another they are found. Learn all you can about a crime scene by looking. Record it, analyze it, and communicate it through artwork. Measure carefully and use a calculator to draw things to scale, if needed.

GRAPH IT! Computer graphics programs make it easy to put your data into graph form for easy viewing and quick communication of your findings to your audience—much better than tables of data or written paragraphs. Check out these websites for making graphs:

- Statistics Canada: http://www.statcan.ca/english/edu/power/ch9/pictograph/picto.htm
- National Center for Education Statistics: www.nces.ed.gov/nceskids/graphing/classic/

POWERPOINT IT! Use a computer to coordinate your graphs, photographs, videos, and other materials into a presentation that's quick to view and easy to understand. You can set up your PowerPoint to loop continually, present it to your teacher on a DVD, and add it to your school portfolio. ***NOTE****: Mac's program Keynote is similar to PowerPoint and works fine, too.*

PHOTOGRAPH IT! Here are some great options:
- still photography
- GIF file. If you have a laptop you can bring for your presentation, use still shots to make a GIF file. The program makes the stills flash by like a flip book, so your viewer sees movement and change.
- Time lapse. When you want to film something that takes place over time, set up the video or still camera to take an image every 30 seconds. The result will be a series of still shots that seem to move and morph over time.
- Microscope photography. Some workshops may require microscopes to view evidence or clues. You can photograph them through

Click

the microscope. Experiment with pointing your camera lens into the eyepiece of your dissecting microscope. You may do just fine this way, but you might have even better luck by using a cell phone camera, because it can lie flush against the eyepiece.

- Flexi-cam is a camera with a magnifying lens, attached to a TV or computer. Viewers can see a tiny bug, a microscopic organism, a water critter, or other things that are alive and in motion, as well as things that aren't. Track down a flexi-cam in your school's science lab or media room, or see if a local university or educational cooperative has one you can borrow.
- Video it. Experiment with different angles if possible, seeing whether things look different from above, from the side, zoomed in, or zoomed out.

the resources

SUPPLIES AND EQUIPMENT

Basic Science Supplies: http://www.basicsciencesupplies.com/
Great Scopes for camera adapter for still photography with microscope: http://www.greatscopes.com/photovideo.htm
USA Scientific: www.usascientific.com
Carolina Biological Supply: http://www.carolina.com
Pillar Scientific: http://www.pillarscientific.com/
Science Stuff: http://www.sciencestuff.com

WEBSITES

- Federal Bureau of Investigation (FBI): http://www.fbi.gov/
- Central Intelligence Agency (CIA): www.cia.gov
- National Institute of Justice: http://www.ojp.usdoj.gov/nij/
- U.S. Department of Homeland Security: http://www.dhs.gov/index.shtm
- The Defense Advanced Research Projects Agency: www.darpa.mil
- Crime Scene Investigator: http://www.crime-scene-investigator.net/
- American Association of Forensic Scientists: www.aafs.org
- Forensics Lab Photo Tour and more from Dr. Henry Lee http://www.drhenrylee.com/
- Young Forensic Scientists Forum www.aafs.org/yfsf/index.htm
- Court TV Crime Library www.crimelibrary.com
- George Washington University Department of Forensic Science: http://www.gwu.edu/~forensic
- American Board of Criminalistics: www.criminalistics.com

BOOKS

- *Forensics for Dummies* by Douglas P. Lyle, John Wiley & Sons Publishers, 2004
- *It's True! This Book Is Bugged* by Sue Bursztynski, Annick Press, 2007
- *Physical Evidence in Forensic Science* by Henry Lee (Lawyers and Judges Publishing, 2000) is the "Bible" of forensics by the leading forensic scientist.

MAGAZINES

- *Forensic Magazine*: http://www.forensicmag.com/articles.asp?pid=120

SCIENCE PROGRAMS FOR KIDS

- Society for Amateur Scientists: www.sas.org

MORE ABOUT PETS

- HomeAgain Pet Recovery Service: www.homeagainid.com
- PETtrac Recovery System: www.advancedidcorp.com
- Pet Hunters International: www.pethunters.com

i Bernstein quote: "Did Somebody Say Indiana Jones?" by Stacey Stowe, the *New York Times,* April 22, 2007.

ii "Traditional Attitudes Toward Bigfoot in Many North American Cultures" by Gayle Highpine, 1995, http://www.bigfootencounters.com/articles/highpine.htm.

iii Ferguson quote: http://www.usu.edu/psycho101/lectures/lectures.htm

iv Ekman quote: "The 43 Facial Muscles That Reveal" by Judy Foreman, the *New York Times,* August 5, 2003.

v Schiro quote: http://www.crime-scene-investigator.net/phoblood.html.

vi Randi quote: "Sleights of Mind" by George Johnson, the *New York Times,* August 21, 2007.

vii The Complete Idiot's Guide to Handwriting Analysis by Sheila R. Lowe, Alpha, 1999, p. 2.

viii *The Andromeda Strain* by Michael Crichton, Alfred A. Knopf, 1969, p. 129.

ix McNair quote: http://www.bbc.co.uk/health/ask_the_doctor/decompositionafterdeath.shtml.

index